Blog

Barely the Beginning

ISHA SANIQUE

authorHOUSE®

AuthorHouse™
1663 Liberty Drive
Bloomington, IN 47403
www.authorhouse.com
Phone: 1-800-839-8640

First published by AuthorHouse 3/25/2011

ISBN: 978-1-4567-5240-8 (e)
ISBN: 978-1-4567-5239-2 (sc)

Library of Congress Control Number: 2011903971

Printed in the United States of America

Dedicated to those who lives are touched by the reading of this blog.

Definitions

Idk (I don't know)

Wtf (what the fuck)

Lol (laugh out loud)

Lmbo (laughing my butt off)

Lmao (laughing my ass off)

Wth (what the hell)

Smdh (shaking my damn head)

Fml (fuck my life)

See I'm really not a big fan of blogs. But everyone keeps telling me I should have one. So although it's not ya typical one here it is.

The demoted fiancé

Girlfriend life is not all it's cracked up to be. Especially when the girlfriend has been demoted from fiancé yes that's me. I got engaged 7 months into my relationship it's never really taken long. March 3rd that day is the day I thought I had finally found that man. Every relationship has problems ours had its share. I'm a back it up a little I met and moved to South Carolina from New Jersey (big difference). Now my decision to move was made within less than a week. I was just so ready to move away from NJ any place would of been fine he could of lived in Wyoming I wouldn't of cared. But ok moved, shortly after the move some very damaging news came to my attention (1 month after) which I should of known it was too good to be true. I'm just so happening to be having a convo with my cousin (first cousin) she tells me yea I'm pregnant blah blah yea I'm happy for her until I ask "who's the father" and she tells me Johnathan. I'm just thinking to myself Johnathan who? Ya know I didn't know I had really asked it out loud. When she said Johnathan Lockett my heart dropped. See Mr. Johnathan Lockett is the dude I moved to South Carolina with. Let alone this dude was sitting right next to me and he knew I was on the phone with her (so what's going thru his head?) He was just playing it so cool like he didn't have a worry in the world.

Ladies, Men please tell me what I already know

Opinions

Soul searcher said…

Girl I don't think I could do it. I don't think I could build on a relationship with it starting off like that... but then again u were kind of stuck out there sooooo... But what was really going thru your mind when your cousin said that he was the baby's father. And what in the hell did u say to him afterwards? Idk wtf I would do in your situation. I think I would have had an empty feeling in my stomach that wouldn't go away... wtf how he just sitting there like you not talking to her though. Idk what I would have done honestly until actually being put in that situation.

Mr. Tell it like it is said...

Wow I think he was maybe thinking like okay since me a her split why not knock her cousin up to maybe rub it in a little. But did your cousin even know you guys were a couple?

Where do I go from here?

Ok now I know what you're going to say, but thing is, I can't tell you anything different than any other woman wouldn't say "I was in love" He became what I knew and I loved it so I stayed. Go ahead get it out I'm messed up for staying cause that was my cousin. Well at the time no, I didn't care I was happy so when he told me it wasn't his and all they had was that one night of course I believed him. Ha-ha. I can't help but to laugh cause I look back at me and say damn I was truly a dumb broad. He had me wrapped around his little finger and I was too green to notice. Actually after that situation was ignored we were happy and connecting on that fiancé level until that glorious day I was born on. Now about a month leading up to my birthday I did notice a slight change in my fiancé's behavior like not answering calls making excuses to go to bed early (oh yea he was working in California I was in South Carolina at the time) saying he didn't feel good he was going to take some medicine and check out for the night (umm hmm) I knew something was up just didn't know what. Now yall know when you truly know and love someone you know just about all there natural habits and daily routines. By heart. I don't think anything could have prepared me for that phone call I got from his side chick on my birthday while we were pulling off from port heading out on our anniversary/my birthday cruise.

Stuck on a boat not knowing what to do...

Opinions

Straight forward and direct said...

OMG, what did she call and say? Ok dumb question, but how did you react to what she said? It's messed up that you were stuck on a boat with his ass. I know that had to be hard. Having to be around each other in the same cabin, same bed. Hat's off to you, I don't think I could have done it.

The payback

So of course it was my turn! All's fair in love and war. Right?

My mind was spinning so hard I was hurt, I was angry and to top it off it was my damn birthday. With all the ideas running through my head should I cheat back (well that's a given) only one thing really stuck out I mean he apologized ya know said all the I don't want to lose you lines so I was gonna make him prove it... I'm a strip away his pride, his manhood, and his dignity, I was gonna make him take it in the ass!

Who said a woman scorned couldn't be ya worst enemy? Nobody, so... what do you think I did?

Opinions

Soul searcher said...

Obviously u must really love this dude cause to stay after that shit.... but then again people do it all the time. Cheat and stay together that is... After u took his manhood did u feel better??? Did it make u feel like he was truly sorry??? Lmao I laugh cause who would have thought about taking a dudes manhood besides nigga in jail. Wow. But ok so what then? How did the relationship change? How is the trust?

Straight forward and direct said…

Okay then, lmao… That is too funny. I take a bow to you… Well done!

Emotions

Ok at the time it did make me feel better and yes it did make me feel as though he was truly sorry. I mean I don't know any man that would allow a woman to get even remotely close to his ass let alone put something in it. And you know what I kind of felt bad afterwards. The relationship did change I cheated he found out and since he's a tic for tac dude he cheated again. After that our relationship has been an uphill downhill battle ever since. Maybe it is time to call it quits. I mean hey I haven't even made it back to being the fiancé yet (it's been over a year)

Left with a big decision to make...

Opinions

Ms. Know a little about a lot said...

Relationships take hard work and both parties have to be committed on making it work. Nothing is worse than finding out the person that you love so much has betrayed you, by not only sleeping with another woman, but the possibility of conceiving with her as well. And what is payback? How can you ever make that person suffer and feel the pain that you felt? Words at that point can only cut so deep! So you go and sleep with someone else... his friend, maybe? Or even worse a family member? But wait, if I cheat, will that make it better? Will that solve the real issue at hand? Will it hurt him like it hurt me? Or will I be "labeled" as hoe, bitch or a slut? Damn! Why did he have to go and do that shit....... will he do it again? Should I leave him? But I love him and it will hurt if I walk away. Hell...I don't even look at him the same. He looks different! Smells different! "Don't touch me", is what I want to tell him. You have had your hands on that other chick and I don't want in parts of that. Cheating is never worth the aftermath that comes with it!

Soul searcher said...

As far as the guy you with... Has the cheating stopped? Because that tit for tat shit gets old. How do u really know that it's done??? Do u ever still have the doubt in your mind that he won't do it? Or that you won't do it? I guess there's a chance people can change. But how can you trust that change was made? I guess as long as you forgive him and vice versa yall will be all good... but still all that is some hard shit to swallow...

Mama drama

A lot of people may say I'm wrong for speaking of my mother this way I mean after all she is my mother so everything I put out I'm doing it with respect lmbo (laughing my butt off)

Ya know I'ma start off by saying maybe it's not her fault I mean she doesn't have the capability of having common sense. Maybe. See my mother has a habit of choosing whatever dude is in at the time over her children. That's just the way she is she is in dire need to be loved by the opposite sex. A woman as pretty as her just doesn't pick the right men. Just recently she got a settlement from an accident $40,000 (yes thousand) do you know she gave all of it to a man she only been knowing for a month when her and her son ain't have a pot to piss in... Now you can guess what that man did right? Yep he disappeared now she looking stupid and feeling foolish. Wtf... I mean tell me what you think... I'ma take it back for another second. My 7th grade year for me was one of the worst years of my life and also the first of the bad memories I have of my mother. She was dating some ol thunder-cat looking guy that drove a blazer. We used to go back and forth to this man's house A LOT. So I took it she really liked this man. So one day they get into an argument and she storms out and leaves me and my little brother there (by the way who does that leave there kids over another man house not there dad after an argument I don't know but my kids would of been leaving when I left) so this man calls me in his room (I'm 70 lbs. soak and wet those who know me know) I go into the room to see what he wanted and he asked me to sit down he wanted to show me something I sit on the bed (no chairs) he closes and locks the door now for some reason he had a top lock on his bedroom door (now that I think about it that's a bit weird) after he locks the door he goes to the top of his closet and pulls out a porno magazine I notice what it is and immediately get up he takes my hand and pushes it down his pants (I'm screaming at this point for my little brother) he wouldn't let me go but God jumped into my lil brother told him to bang on the door screaming to let me out. My brother saved my life that day I am forever grateful to you for that Thank You! He let me out and took us home. Immediately I said mom I have to tell you something but when he leaves, she made me tell her right then and I did and she went off and when she went off I wasn't scared anymore it left me she was my hero seriously. 2 days later she was going out with him again my heart sank literally I didn't know what to think I guess she really didn't believe me...

That's the day I lost all respect for that woman who birthed me.

Believe it or not that's not even the bad part that comes in when she decides to have a convo with my fiancé at the time (I had already told him the story) he just asked her about it because she was working for his mom and talking about us terrible to the other employees (and she lived with us) so he asked her about it do you know what she told him she told him that me (70 lbs. soak and wet) came on to that man and he pushed me off of him while saying No Stop I'm in love with ya mother!

Come the hell on yall wtf... I'm hurt I'm heartbroken (I'm on 3 way)

What to do?

I put her ass out of my house to think that of me all these years I'm 30 now. I was 13 then. She had to go...

I mean what should I have done? She had it embedded in her head that that is exactly what happened. And from my tears of disbelief to screaming to the top of my lungs that's all she wanted to believe.

But I still forgave her... Big mistake! Can't teach an old dog new tricks...

Opinions

Soul searcher said...

My mom and I have our issues, well really no issues because we don't talk now. But I definitely understand where you're coming from. I don't think I would have tried so many times to be nice to my mom...for her to hurt u sooooo many times. You have a big heart!!!! You have to let that go though... Forgive and release... That will make you a better person. Not saying rebuild a relationship, but let it go so u can live at piece...

Straight forward and direct said…

Normally I would say that you need to mend that with your mom. But it seems like every time you give her another chance she ends up hurting you worse than before. She seems to be set in her ways. Honestly if she has been that way this long I don't think there is room for her to change. That's just going to be her so you can either chose to deal with it or not and just let it go. Unless she went through some extensive counseling there is no hope for that situation. My opinion you're better off without her. Matter of fact anything that causes you that much hurt isn't good for you and you should let it go.

Food for thought...

Everyone has problems I'm well aware of that. I'm not saying mine are worse or better. I think it's not the problems you have it's how you get through and deal with the problems you have. That's what makes you that strong and undeniable individual. Love yourself first and know your own self-worth (which should be priceless) cause if you don't everyone else won't either! Those who encourage you are those you shouldn't forget!

The break up

So today I woke up feeling like crap I really didn't get much sleep for one my air mattress sprung a leak secondly me and my boyfriend broke up last night. Crazy thing is, is that we live together. After 4 years of back and forth make up to break ups I think this one is the final episode. He blew up on me about an argument we had a week prior. The argument was about me wanting a puppy. Right, I'm not even going to get on how petty it was. But obviously it wasn't petty to him. From what he told me he had been contemplating ending it all week. (Breaking up that is) To me it sounds like bull shit. I think he has a backup plan to be honest somewhere or there's someone else he'd rather be with. I don't know but I'm torn I know I said that I wanted it to be over but now that it is I don't know if that's what I want. I'm confused and I really don't want to lose him. I don't know if it's because I have to see him every day or if I just genuinely want him in my life. How are we going to survive in one house and not being in a relationship.

Is this a recipe for disaster?

Opinions

Soul searcher said...

Well that was a dumb reason to be breaking up, but do people need a reason these days... if yall break up over a puppy, then what next???

Family/Spouse

I tried to reach out to my sister even though after what she did she should have been reaching out to me. Oh yall don't know huh... Well sit down for this one...

My father called me and asked me to drive to Atlanta with him to pick up my sister and my two brothers they were moving to Virginia to live with him for a while. On our way back from Atl we had a discussion to see if my sister could come and stay with me for the first week. Yae I was excited and so was she but for other reasons. Skipping forward my dad agrees and the week she's there we have a blast she's connecting with my kids everything is everything. June 23rd was her last day there. We even went to king's dominion that weekend she left. The week had been nice.

So on July 5th I'm a little confused I had been calling and calling her and my dad but no one was answering my calls. 3 days later I had a detective call my house asking to speak to my kids' father. Now I don't know who she thought she was dealing with but I'm a ride or die so even though he was lying right next to me I told her he wasn't there and asked her what was the nature of her call. She responds by saying it has to do with my sister. So I'm like why the hell are you calling here for him about MY sister. "You have to take that up with them she says". Like... what? What the hell you mean take it up with them. Ok, immediately I woke him up (after hanging up) asking why the hell was a detective calling him about my sister he say I don't know is she in some kind of trouble or something.

Now come on yall was he seriously trying to play me with that bogus-ness of an answer??

Opinions

Soul searcher said

Well what the hell was the detective calling for then...damn shame u can't even trust ya man let alone your own family.... Makes u think who really on your damn side...

What the

After a week of trying to get in touch with my dad and my sister. Oh and not getting any answers out of my kids father. The detective calls my house AGAIN asking for him. At this point I'm fed up with guessing what the hell is going on. I tell her she will get no more cooperation from me until she tells me what's going on. That's when the bomb hit me. She tells me that my sister is accusing my kid's father of raping her. I dropped the phone. My suspicions on what was going on turned out to be true. Although I had the feeling of that being it her actually saying and confirming it felt like my world had just died. I couldn't believe it. I didn't know what to do or how to react. I started thinking back to that week she was there trying to remember something anything that would tie that together. Why hadn't I noticed it? Or sensed it? I couldn't remember anything being out of place.

(Recalling thoughts)

I went downstairs twice that night to wake him up. He was drunk sleeping sitting up on one couch she was sleeping on the other one. I went downstairs the first time because I had to fix my son a bottle I tried to wake him up then. The second time I went downstairs because I woke up and noticed he still hadn't come to bed. This time he got up and came upstairs. Ok next morning a lot of laughing I recall her asking him if he was going to Kings Dominion with us. Nothing seemed out of place. I've went over this a million and one times. Still things seemed weird. Finally my talk with her... It seemed as though her focus was off from what I was asking her all she kept saying was "I told you, you should have left him a while ago. You're going to stay with him and take his side over mine." When all I'm trying to do is find out what happen. I felt like I was pleading with her to tell me what happen. Why didn't she kick the table yell out my name? Something. I was right upstairs. I know people handle things differently but no way in this world would I be laughing and joking with a man that just RAPED me the night before. Things ended badly after that. Somehow it ended with a threat and me canceling myself out of the whole situation. I didn't know what else to do I had three kids to survive for. I couldn't put myself in the middle. So I did what was best for them, what was best for me. I cut both of them off cold turkey.

Opinions

Straight forward and direct said…

I know you had kids by this man but I think you should have stuck by your blood. If you have been through it then you can imagine how she was feeling and what she was battling. After a tragedy like that she must have felt abandoned by you. She may have even blamed you. This situation can only be whole again with God as the mediator. I know you feel betrayed and you did what you thought was best. No one can fault you for that. It may have been the best decision at the time. How are you guys now? Have yall came to mends? How is you and your kid's father's relationship?

Soul searcher said

This is why females have issues with each other. You can't even trust your own sister.... this is why I stay to myself. Again how do you find it in your heart to trust anyone? I hope you know I would never do that to you. I'm still smdh about it all.

A day in court

The detective came to search my house for my kid's father a couple days later. Me I'm still in disbelief. So when she ask me what has he told me. I say that he didn't do it. She responds by saying " well if he didn't do it why does he have the same two STD's that your sister has. I was horrified. All I could think of was 3 kids later and two STD's. Oh hell no. I didn't know what to do so my mom was in the house I left and started walking. To where I don't know I just started walking. To my surprise he was coming down the street. With the officers watching me the whole time I walk in front of his car yelling and screaming at him and for some reason I warn him that the police were at the house searching for him. Why did I do that? This confirmed that yea he did do what she said he did. I went to the hospital, turns out I didn't have anything. Her whole case was based upon him giving her the STD's which was impossible because I didn't have anything. In court when the doctor testified that I didn't have anything she took the stand and said it was consensual and that they had, had sex back in March when she came down to visit. Wtf?

Why me? Bitter and broken...

Opinions

Straight forward and direct said

OH hell nah, are you serious after all that she comes out and says it was consensual. That would have been an ass whipping waiting to happen. So what then how are you and your sister now? I don't even think I would ever want to talk to her again after that. And I honestly think that I would be fine with it. That's a big issue. But then again you two are blood so yall need to work that out. No man children or no children should come between yall. Family can do you even dirtier than friends which is a damn shame. I know the feeling. But nothing good ever comes out of staying mad at each other it's not just yall two that suffers it's the children too, some way or another.

Making a mends

Six years has gone by since the last time I've spoken to or even seen my sister. I felt as though it was time to right my wrongs with her. My dad and I had been talking so I asked him if he could give her my phone number. Every time I asked him or brought her up he always found a way to change the subject. So I kind of got tired of it and I asked him... "Do you blame me for what happened to my sister?" He tried to get out of the question by saying he didn't want to talk about it right then. But no we were going to talk about it if not then, then when? It had been six whole years already going on seven. That day was going to be the day to talk. To my surprise but not really he told me yes. Yes he did blame me. He blamed me because he says I should have known what type of person I was in a relationship with (but people live with murderers all their lives and don't know the bodies are buried under the house... if you get what I mean) It broke my heart. All these years have gone by we talk not a lot but enough. For this whole time him to blame me. Wow... I was furious. I couldn't help but to cry and tell him it wasn't my fault. I was hurting in all this too. My sister was not the only victim in this situation. My whole life was changed due to that incident. Why couldn't he see that? Why couldn't he understand that? It wasn't up to him whether or not my sister and I talked it was her decision. I still think he blames me even after I pleaded my case. But he did end up giving me her number. Which now I kind of wish he hadn't. Long story short we both were not ready. It ended up being a disaster. I don't know what I expected. But now I'm okay with how things are even if there non-existent.

Opinions

Straight forward and direct said…

Yes, maybe they are better off that way. Why reopen closed wounds. I don't think no one will truly know the truth in what happened. I think both parties still have information which they choose not to disclose. It's probably for the best. For the sake of your sanity. Just leave it in God's hands it's his battle now.

Soul searcher said

Ok… its a shame that your family doesn't see things the way you want them to. Your dad decided he was going to believe what your sister said. To me that wasn't right because he only heard one side. They say you should be able to count on your family, but time after time you have been shown that you can't. Don't let that keep you down. You know who you can count on though.

Dumb, dazed, and confused

Lawd, why do I put myself through these dumb relationships and I know there dumb. But yet I let them continue. I'm starting to wonder if I just like the hurt. Like ok two days ago (I know when they say when you go looking you shall surely find) so my dude left his phone on the bed (already yall know) yes I went through it. And of course I seen something that set me off into a dumb mood. Here this dude was asking some other chick if she was ready for him (sexually) yea of course the bitch said yes that mess touched me made me feel so hurt so I asked him about it (do you know what this (bleep) told me. "I was just talking junk to the broad. Maybe I should of put LOL behind my bad won't happen again besides that's (what cha ma-call-it's broad)" ok then so then why today I ask to use this (bleeps) phone and

YES I went through it again and this time I see naked pics of this donkey (apparently he asked her to send them when he texted her to call his ass) I know ya thinking wtf is it that I'm confused about I see the bull in black and white! Right I do. But my mind set is so ON right now I can't help but want to blow his mind for I leave. Time out; I'm bout to first be on some get fine ish, stack some money ish, and use the hell outta his ass. I prayed about it of course but I think the dark angle had the last say on this one...

Opinions

Straight forward and direct said...

LEAVE HIM! That's the only thing you need to be considering doing. All that extra ish is for the birds. It seem like you using payback as a reason to stay. Idk I would of been gone the strong woman I am this just speaks volumes about your character... If you portray weak that's how you'll be treated... I'm just saying.

Tight as tube socks

I've loved the worst and the best of them. And maybe both at the same time. What do I be getting myself into? Earlier I told u about the demoted fiancé. The cousin ordeal well here's my half of the fault. So I met this dude back when I was working in the strip club (bartending don't get it twisted) but fine this dude with a swag nobody could touch. Jowell was his name. Now when I met him I was working I didn't know what he drove none of that all I knew is he had a slick tongue and was good with words. Skipping forward we kicked it hard for about 4 months hard as in he was basically living with me. Yes I gave him the key. I ended up driving cross country with this dude thinking in a couple weeks I would be living there. (Where's a needle so I can pop my own bubble). This was his home so he introduced me to some family some friends and some co-workers. Well one of his friends was Johnathan (yes Mr. Lockett) I know what you're thinking but at that time I was so gone over Jowell I won't paying attention to them other people I couldn't have told you how they looked the next day. Well when it came time for me to move dude flaked on me changed his number just left me high and dry. I didn't understand and again I was confused and hurt I mean I didn't have any explanation on why. I had nothing. So when I met Johnathan I had no clue who he was. I worked in a strip club I see so many dudes if you look familiar I'm going to assume that's where I know you from. Me and Johnathan got tight engaged even as you know. Well around the time I found out about my cousin was about the time I found out about him and Jowell being damn near best friends they were (tight as tube socks) co-workers that traveled together. Recently Jowell's mom facebooked me. I knew exactly who she was although I had never met her in person. I ended up with Jowell's number by the end of our convo. I know I shouldn't of but yes I called I felt as though (yes even though I'm dating his close friend) I still needed an explanation on why he left me like that. From there he told me he missed me. I told you he had a way with words right. How could I let him suck me back in again. I should have known it was a set up, but I couldn't resist talking to him. (Huge mistake) Yea he was always good with words which meant he was also good at running his mouth this dude went and told a mutual friend of theirs everything (strategy he knew the friend would go back and tell my dude).

How am I going to get out of this one? Boy, do I have my blonde moments...

Opinions

Soul searcher said...

Wow.... a small world huh. Did u ever get closer though??? Cause all it seemed like to me was more fucking drama. How could u explain that one when Jonathan asked you about it? For real though I don't think I would have kept fucking with either... Jonathan knew who u was...that's messed up. Lol we say we adults, but in the end still kind of play childlike games...lol

Tic for Tac

A big blow up is what I got but somehow he forgave me. Well actually I felt he had no choice especially with all I had been through with his ass. But as you know I have a tic for tac dude so I knew with him it wasn't over.

Yes I did it even though I know he hates it and would blow up if he found out but I went through his phone that night. He decided to blow off some steam and go to the club that night. Now before he goes to the club we were chillin no beef sitting watching one of his favorite TV shows. His phone starts going off after the first text he decides to put his phone on silent. (Ok then) I guess he thinks I'm deaf dumb and blind. I knew he would come in that night pissy drunk and he did. That was my chance when he was dead drunk asleep. What I read in his text messages blew my damn mind so I quickly jotted her number down and decided to speak to her myself. After a couple text messages she agrees to meet me the next morning...

I wasn't prepared for this one... She told me everything I didn't want to hear of course.

Opinions

Soul searcher said...

I don't think I would be meeting any chicks... that's crazy. But u ain't me either. And still after all that u still decide to work it out with him....is all that drama worth it? Are you just settling??

Straight forward and direct said...

I don't think you should of went there. Why do you feel as though you had to meet her? What to see if she was as pretty as you? To see if she stacked up to your standards? Would you have felt better if she was ugly? What purpose did it serve to meet her face to face? You did know that she wasn't going to come with good news, didn't you? I feel as though in situations like that it just put you off in a bad place. You got the answers you needed when you read the text messages. Why you needed her to justify them in person Idk. I think it's time for you to start focusing on yourself putting so much energy into a relationship that seems to be bringing so much hurt and pain seems to be holding you back. The real focus needs to be on yourself and your babies.

Stressed up bringing

Looking back, I didn't have the best childhood. But even though I didn't I did have some good memorable moments. My grandmother raised me cause my mother liked to party and do drugs. Living with my grandmother was rough. See my grandma didn't play. I was quiet growing up really quiet. So quiet my nick name was turtle (they say cause I used to be off in my own little shell.) With 12 grandchildren in the house I know it must have been very stressful for my grandmother. I guess she figured she had to take her stress out on someone, why not us. No matter what it was if she could pick it up, if she could throw it, it was going to connect with you. I can remember a time when I was five just learning how to put on my own clothes. Only thing is, I forgot my underwear and my cousin told on me. The normal thing to do is to explain to the child the right way to dress themselves without punishment. No, she chose a different approach. She grabbed my no, no place (my private) pinched, twisted, and lifted me up to my toes and told me if she ever caught me without any underwear again she would snatch it off.

(Grandma… I was 5. I didn't know. I promise I didn't.)

Not getting into all of the incidences there were times when I wished myself dead. Or that my mom or dad would come and take me. I got my wish all too soon. My sixth grade year someone from social services had visited my school. They came to talk to me. I already knew they would my grandmother had told us they were coming one day she didn't know when. But she had us prepped and ready. See she lived by the Vegas rule… What happens in that house stays in that house. She told us if we said something they would take us away to a foster home where they would give us to men that would abuse our bodies and our minds. But talking to the social service lady she told me something completely different and I believed her. She told me I would go to live with my dad. And she was right.

I was free…

Opinions

Straight forward and direct said…

(tears…) I wish I could have saved you back then. I wish I was your super-hero. I'm so sorry that I wasn't strong enough to help you through it. But I was a kid too. I know all the sadness you have inside of you didn't just happen overnight. And even though I checked out most of the time I was there for all of it… I wish I was strong enough to help. Because what she did to you she did to me too. As is with everything else.

Self we will get through it… I promise you we will…

Soul searcher said...

You had a messed up childhood. Makes me want to tear up. But I say again…. you would not be you if you didn't go through all of that. Not to say it was right back then, but that made u the strong person I see today. Do you and grandma have a better relationship since

you are an adult now? How has all the failed
relationships with your family effected you?

Love and respect

My grandmother is bed ridden now and about 800 lbs. plus. It hurts me to see her that way and then again I feel it's what she deserves. But truth is no one deserves that. You know I love her as though she never did anything bad to me at all. Family don't hardly go around anymore. When we were younger she was the one that kept us together even though she was mean, abusive, (verbally and physically) she gave me the greatest gift I could of ever asked for. The gift of learning how to become a strong woman. I can't imagine how hard it must of been on her to have to take care and raise all of her adult kids children. I take my bow to her. Despite everything what I see most in her is an amazing woman, that above all cost just wanted to keep her family together.

Opinions

Straight forward and direct...

I commend you for looking beyond the hurt and pain and giving respect to that who raised you. Probably the best way she knew how. It's hard being mad at someone for so long holding a grudge against them it only makes you miserable. You have proved to be that amazing woman you say she is just by that situation comment alone.

Feeling used...

You all know about the kids father and my sister. I'm over that but how many of you have ever felt like (now some may relate and some may not) but have you ever felt like a used slut. Here's what I mean. I wasn't working my kids father and I were going through that whole thing with him and my sister shit. My kids needed things bills needed to be paid. I could call my kids father and be like the kids have a couple diapers left can you bring some by. His response would be "if you give me something" (as if referring to some ass). I cursed him the hell out. Like are you serious I'm telling you your 3 children need diapers and you worried bout some oochie! Like, wtf... Well after 3 days of no shows, no calls, no nothing... I gave in. It was crazy how everyone treated me as if it were my fault he slept with my sister. I hated myself I hated him for doing that to me and for me allowing it. I felt like a used in every way slut... Emotionally, physically, sexually... I was at a low this man that has shared six years and three kids with me slept with my sister (and someone else in my family that I didn't know about before. I'll touch on that later). He had used me up. Like a dingy dish towel. I felt trapped, I didn't know a way out of this situation... Until I met Paul... I had the mind frame to replace the love I had for someone else. Yea, Not the brightest of ideas...

Opinions

Straight forward and direct said...

No, definitely not the brightest idea. That was a recipe for disaster before it even started. On the kids father situation I've been there the key thing is I didn't stay there and I didn't use another man to pick me back up. I used that thing God gave me called "Faith". That's what you needed. I'm just saying...

Soul searcher said...

Shit... I really don't know what to say. The kids father is grimey as hell and so are the family members. S/N in life we all have done things that we hate ourselves for...understand that it made u feel like a used slut..you were young and didn't know what else to do at the time. Now you can look back and say wtf was I thinking...so lesson learned. As far as replacing love that you had for someone else...that is a natural action in this type of situation. Just know that the new, so-called, love doesn't always work because you are still damaged for what you just went through.

Keeping it in the family

So in finding out that my kids father slept with my sister on more than one occasion. It also came out that he had had relations with another cousin of mine. Now get this its the same cousin that now has the baby by my dude. Jerry Springer-ish huh. I know. Of course when I asked her about it she denies it. Oh and to answer a question before asked NO I didn't do it for pay back. Even though I feel wronged in every way when it comes to a man. Off situation even my mom. Ok I lost my virginity at 17 1/2. The man I lost it to was 24 at the time. This dude had swag for days. Dark chocolate and sexy. Well what I liked in him so did my mother. Ultimately I really don't know if she took it to that level with him or not. I guess now after all this time it really doesn't matter. But what's crazy is how small this world is because that dude now works with the tight as tube socks niggas. Yes they know each other. FML! This is starting to sound like damn a soap opera.

Opinions

Straight forward and direct said...

OMG... Yes it is soap opera central. Like wtf is wrong with family all these dudes out here, its more than enough to go around. Why you would need to share or trade like we are in short supply of men is beyond me.

Soul searcher said...

Man... all that is summed up in one word... "JEALOUSY". Why else would the family want to be or should I say sleep with all the men you are with. I mean come on you can't get your own man??

Mother over-protective

Those who have children know how it can be when it comes to someone messing with your child. Well those who don't or do, I'ma voice my fiasco's I've had the oh so pleasure of experiencing. So I have 3 children I take pride in them, I love them and most of the time I feel as though they are all I have in life. I can be a little protective at times. Here's what I mean...

School bus oh hell nah!!

After I put my mother out she had "no place to go" she was homeless so she says (somehow her cell phone stayed charged... Hmm). So my little brother stayed with me with a two week maximum stay. See I had to do that cause my mother is the type to take advantage of situations like that she'll disappear then I'd be basically stuck.

(Message alert: To all my other family its your turn I've taken care of them for the last 7 years she has other children and other siblings yall do something for a change). Not to jump off subject but my brother that's right beneath me told me it was my job my responsibility to take care of them like are you serious I have 3 babies he doesn't have any... Do the math huh...

Anyway one day I was picking my brother up from school he was in the 8th grade. We just so happen to end up riding along side his old school bus. Well I had all my kids in the car. My middle daughter which is blonde curly hair with blue-grey eyes was looking up at the kids on the bus (who were acting a damn fool). Kids were yelling and screaming all out the windows they were out of they're seats like wtf... I've driven school buses before and there is no way I would of let them act they way, they would of been finding there own way to school. So my daughter had looked down (she's 8 at the time) and a little boy said "hey lil girl" when she didn't look back up he said "well fuck you then you white bitch". I was furious now at first I tried to sike myself out so I asked my daughter was she okay. She was like mommy that boy just called me a white B (now mind you my daughter thinks she's peach). So I told her, nah baby I don't think he was talking to you. My daughters face was so flush red her eyes were teary. That's when I snapped/blacked out. See my daughter think she's peach. She doesn't do black and white. Quick example true story.

(Sorry off subject)

I tried to explain to my daughter the different races that she has all mixed up in her and she literally told me I was silly because she's peach and that there's no way she could be black and white. So we were in 7-11 one day and a lady walked in with vitiligo (for those who don't know that's when you have light colored blotches on your skin) anyway my daughter said to me out the blue "see mommy I told you I wasn't black and white, she's black and white I'm peach! OMG, talking bout embarrassed. Horrified at the fact that I almost bursted out laughing. All seriousness though I just wanted to point out how my daughter perceives color/ races hence why I was so upset at that child's ignorance. I'm just saying...

Getting back on subject... I started honking

my horn at the bus so that it could pull over but she kept driving. So I eased my vehicle into that lane so that she had no choice but to pull over on the sidewalk. When she did I pulled over and parked in front of her. Got my daughter out the car and we walked up to the bus doors. (Lawd forgive me) I knocked on the bus doors and she looked at me as if I was crazy (she thought right), not budging so I spoke up (DON'T TRY THIS AT HOME) and said if you don't open this door the next time I tap on it its gonna be with my pistol. To my surprise the dummy opened the door, cause I would of let my crazy ass sit out there and I would of peeled off on my ass. LOL. When I stepped on the bus I addressed the bus driver...

"This is dammit ridiculous there is no reason for these dam kids to be acting like this out they seats cursing and throwing shit out the windows I drove buses and every last one of them would of been hitching rides with they mama's or the city bus. They should be more afraid of you then you are of them WTF type operation yall running down here"...

Then I addressed the chir-en...

"I'ma tell ya this, this one right chea this one mine right chea. Naan one a yall even whisper something out ya mouth you go be calling ya mama and daddy's to meet me at the school yard tomorrow, Cause I'm bout to fuck one a they kids up whisper something I dare you!

(I know yall that may have been a bit much)

But... All those kids that were cursing, yelling, and throwing shit out the window were quiet as church mice. I didn't feel bad afterward sorry I just didn't. But I did want to know how my daughter felt. So when we got home I asked her how it made her feel. Do you know what she told me "uh mommy I kinda wish uh I kinda wish I would of not said anything" like wtf... Now you know the ignorance came back out for a sec. So I told her "see now... that's, that white people shit" LMAO!

Opinions

Straight forward and direct said...

Ok you are too much I don't know whether to laugh or be flabbergasted at the fact that you that reckless with kids but I feel where you coming from so in the end I'm LMAO!

Real as can be said...

Well...I, myself would have probably said the same thing as your daughter...I guess that's my white side talking too. Lmao. But girl yo ass crazy at times. You got your point across though huh? Lol. The things we do to protect our children. SMDH...

CPS neighbors

Ya know time had passed since that school bus blackout with dealing with my kids. Ya know even though I made a joke out of it I've tried to take heed to what my daughter said. Which brings me to this situation...

I have these neighbors that stay semi beneath us. Just so happen one of the neighbors bedroom is right under my kids rooms. (Whoops for you). LOL. So 1st day we moved in he was a jerk. We back an forth moving things in I'm not knowing if there's assigned parking ya know. So we are in the house putting up stuff... Moving in. Neighbor pulls up gets out the car and yells out "stop parking in my fucking spot". Ime-ge-itly (immediately) I went outside and asked him O my bad is there assigned parking or something? He responded

"No". So like dude wtf is ya problem. He was like "O I'm just being an asshole". I left it alone. The woman in me left it alone. Now I don't know what he had against us but I've never had a neighbor play there music so loud it sounds like I'm sitting front row live. I kept my cool. One Saturday morning at about almost 6 a.m. I get awakened to all this cursing yelling bumping just some bull ish. The craziness woke my kids up. So you know I didn't get any sleep right. Ok bout 9:17 a.m. I get a knock on my door. Its my neighbor he came to ask me if I can tell my kids to quiet down so that he can get some sleep. I'm like are you serious you woke them up at bout 6 this morning now at almost ten you want me to ask them to quiet down... The whole time I'm thinking role model, be civilized. I said ok. Yes I really did say ok. 2 nights later it snowed they closed schools but I still had to work. I a.m. to 8 p.m. My dude called me at 5 p.m. and said the neighbors left a note on the door and I wasn't gonna like it. He told me I was gone snap off. Now him saying that I already had a clue on what it said.

"Dear neighbors,

Please stop with all this stomping, heavy-footed walking, jumping, indoor horseplay,etc. I have asked nicely a time before and noticed my request has went unresolved. This is childish, rude, and very disrespectful of you as a neighbor and as a parent. There is a playground up the street on the right exersize there, not on top of our roof. It wakes us up keeps us from sleeping and enjoying activities. It also stresses out my pet. Please grow up and respect this simple request.

(P.S. Unattended children will be reported to C.P.S.)"

...Now you can almost do whatever to me and it wouldn't make me flinch... But... When it comes to my kids, (SMDH). Now the whole body of that mess didn't mean a hill of beans to me when I read the P.S. part. I flipped out... Badly. I went over civilized and basically said "I'ma tell ya this those are my kids and if they are neglected I welcome you to call C.P.S. But if you can hear them laughing, playing, and exersizing on ya roof they are in no way neglected. So you can keep that bullshit and learn ya damn laws cause there is no legal age limit to let a child(ren) stay home alone in this particular state. Life and bills don't stop cause mother nature gave my kids a snow day". He had the nerve to raise his voice at me and was like don't you fuking curse at me.

Like wtf... and I said dude I came over here civilized but what I'm bout to do is just haul off and steal off on ya ass... I blacked out from there. My dude ended up picking me up and carrying me in the house. Lesson learned for the neighbor... Hmm...

Opinions

What in the world said...

I know it can be overwhelming when it comes to kids and protecting them I feel you. But you have to find your calm and let God handle the rocky. You gotta problem handing over that burden. Find peace within yourself and some trust in God that he gone work it out...

Family... Something...

I wanna start this one off by saying I do wish things and family were different but I was put in the midst of these people for a reason. That reason is still a mystery to me. Family can be an amazing thing and the worst. The men in my family I pray to God don't have daughters. My 7th grade year was literally one of the worst years of my life that year alone my moms boyfriend now just baby daddy put a knife to my neck all because I went to a school dance. Guess what my mother did as she stood there and watched him do it? Nothing, she did absolutely nothing. That contributed to the loss of respect I had for her. Not only that one morning I woke up to my older cousin pushing himself inside me... Even his dad would touch me every time he came around or if I walked past him. I quickly learned to try and keep my distance. But he always found ways to work his way by me. Then he would be like Oh my bad or excuse me I aint see you... WTF ever! Sad part is since when my mom didn't believe me bout what her dude did to me bout a month earlier, I was afraid of not being believed this time too. So I kept it to myself. Until... My facebook blow up. See my family loves drama. My mother for some reason likes to just talk bad about me sort of like jealousy if you ever heard her. She told all this crazy stuff to the family that I had never even heard of before. I'm like dude when did that happen like example she told them when my brother was a baby I took a hot fork and pressed it against his face burning him. WTF!! Like when did this happen? Why didn't she whip my ass? Why have I never heard anything about this before today? I have nooo idea where she got that from how she even thought that up. I seriously think something is mentally disturbing about her.

Opinions

Always standing strong said...

Man, I don't know if I could have handled all of that. I feel sad for children that have to live in environments like that. People are sick. I know that probably makes you that much more protective over your kids... I understand your hurt I understand your anger. So I say vent and let it out. As long as positive comes from it then greatness is possible. Let all parts of life be lessons taught and most of all lessons learned...

Ms. Possibility said...

I pitty anyone who reads this and feels sorry. Because what you have become what you've turned around and made out of your experience is a masterpiece. You a strong woman with three beautiful and still amazing children. I envy you... You are truly a portrait of all things being possible... That's my opinion with all the craziness.

Rock bottom
(life announcement)

I don't know if anyone of you have ever felt as though you done hit rock bottom I hit mine about 6 months ago. My dude and I called it quits and being as though I lived with him I had to move out so I did I went back to NJ. Everything was good at first I bought me a new truck 3 days after I got there the same day I got the truck I landed a job. It was looking as though the split was a good decision made. At that time me and my kids were living with my kid's nana (their father's mom... long story... Lol). A couple days go by I'm excited to be starting a job. Especially so soon. I get a text message stating that one of the owners had promoted a waitress to the job position I was to have. That was okay though cause I had already landed another one. Only thing is I had to settle for a lesser position. It was a job and I needed it. Things are going ok so one day I get back from getting groceries and my kids nana is cursing and calling my kids profane words now that's a no no but before I could find out what was truly going on we ended up getting into it. Which led to me being homeless...

That went too far... Look what it got me...

I never intended for that to happen but who does in that situation. I worked out a deal with her so that at least during the week when I couldn't afford a hotel that at least my kids could sleep there. That turned out to be all week except weekends. I found myself sleeping in my truck some nights at a friend's house. It became easier just to sleep in my truck. On this night I decide I'm staying at my friend's house. Hoping she would be up I didn't get off work till round 2:30 sometimes 3. I pull up get out and while walking up the grassy hill I dropped my keys. I'm kneeling down looking for them when I hear two men behind me... (If this ain't rock I don't know what is).

Fast forward... I ended up in the hospital that night.

I felt like I had nothing left they had taken my body from me I had no home for my kids or money for a hotel social services was giving me the run around. Soon after that I quit my job just from being so scared of being raped again. I felt useless to myself and everyone around me. I tried it... I let go of the steering wheel and told God to drift me I don't want to feel this pain anymore. He kept my truck driving straight. Now I know I needed an alignment but as the curb bent so did my truck. It wasn't my time.

I have kids! I have life! What was I thinking?...

Opinions

Straight forward and direct said…

Sometimes in order to get ahead you have to learn when to talk and when to just keep it to yourself. You have to learn how to make the best out of a bad situation even though it's hard, it may be worth it in the end. The last thing a mother or father wants is for their children to be out on the streets with nowhere to go. It's called biting the bullet. Where is your family? Why aren't they helping? Do they know what's going on?

Life Announcement...

If you are being or were victimized by anyone you can talk to someone. You need to talk to someone. From experience it won't stop eating at you until you do. You take it in every situation every relationship whether male or female. It takes a toll on your mind your spirit and your soul. Get help. It's easy to hide hurt but hard as hell to hide happy. Someone will listen...

Opinions

Soul searcher said...

Wow...as I sit here and process all that I'm am speechless. No one deserves all of that. Makes u kind of think, who can u really trust who can u turn to in time of need. Well just know thru all that a much strong woman came out of it. I am truly sorry about what all u had to go thru, but they say sometimes u have to hit rock bottom before things change for the better. You are a very strong woman, but u r not your mother at all. Keep your head up. God has your back.

One great friend
(you know who you are)

I have to give thanks to you. You were there when I didn't have anyone else. With no hesitation you gave me and my children a place to stay. You wouldn't take no for an answer. I love you for that. Thank you for always making me laugh, especially when times were at their worst. Right from jump street we had a special bond I am forever grateful to you...

Wake up call....

When I look back over all that has happen since me and my ex split I think if I would of stayed none of this would have happened maybe I should go back to where I know I'll be safe. So here I am. Why does it seem so hard to let go? Why do I keep finding excuses to come back? Happy to soon to be miserable... I know what to expect but yet I still put myself and my children through it. Am I my mother's daughter? Am I that anxious to be loved by the opposite sex? Why do I feel like I'm describing her? I've lost myself somewhere its time I get back to the basics, time I retract my steps. But then again... No, that's my problem always wanting to work backwards... It's time to move forward and move on...

Last thought...

Someone told me that even though I may see some similarities I am not my mother. You know what? You are so right! Through all the trails, the errors. Through the hopeful and the let downs. I'm still here, and much stronger than before.

I am my children's mother and I am a child of God... So now, I stand to rise...

Day dreaming and thinking of making me happy...

(Is this the end of a bitter chapter?...)

Until the next blog...